DEDICATION

To the
Jewish People
on whose lives
these poems are based.

—

ACKNOWLEDGEMENTS

I would like to thank Gerald Davis
for his valued advice and support.
I would also like to thank Robert Greacen
and Fred Johnston.

I wish to acknowledge my debt to the following two books
which provided inspiration for this collection of poems:

The Jews of Ireland - From Earliest Times to the Year 1910,
by Louis Hyman, Irish University Press, 1972.

A Short History of the Jews in Ireland,
by Bernard Shillman, 1945.

The poems, *Marcus Harfman* and *Benny Bloom,*
were previously published in Books Ireland and
The Burning Bush respectively.

FOREWORD

Perhaps it is the happy fact that Irish Jews have never suffered as their co-religionists in other countries that has been counterproductive to the creation of a dynamic that might have produced a great writer from our community.

It took James Joyce, an Irish Catholic, to invent Leopold Bloom. Gerry McDonnell has been similarly moved to write about his Jewish neighbours. In his case, as he points out, his interest was motivated first by curiosity. As he looked deeper into the history of a forgotten corner of his city he was moved to write about a world that was both familiar and foreign to a Dubliner. We are fortunate that, in doing so, he created a series of imaginative and fascinating vignettes that conjure up a poignant perspective of what must have been a unique and idiosyncratic society.

Dublin Jewry has changed much over the years. There is no Jewish area as such, no "Little Jerusalem" with the characters who once enlivened South Circular Road. The era of Ballybough cemetery is even further removed from the community of today. Gerry McDonnell has done what only a poet can do - he has brought the dead alive. In doing so, he has preserved in the amber of his poetry, a period of our history which, to our eternal loss, we could too easily have forgotten.

Gerald Davis

CONTENTS

INTRODUCTION

I grew up in an area of Dublin which was reclaimed from the sea. The old name for this locality is Mud Island. At present it comprises the neighbourhoods of Fairview and across the river Tolka, of Ballybough. On Fairview Strand, where at one time the sea lapped the shore, is a curious house with a more curious date over the door. As a child I wondered at this date which reads 5618. I wondered was it 1856 in reverse. The puzzle over that date, cut in stone, remained unsolved for me until recent times. I discovered that the house is the caretaker's house for a Jewish cemetery which lies behind it.

The date 5618 is the year in the Jewish calendar which corresponds with 1858 in the Christian calendar. It is recorded that after 1700 the number of Jews in Dublin increased. They were forbidden to purchase land within the city, so they leased this plot of land to serve as a cemetery, beyond the river Tolka which marked the Municipal boundary. It is interesting to note that this marshland area corresponds to the Marais (marsh) district where Jews settled in Paris. The Jewish cemetery at Ballybough was not exclusively for Dublin Jews and so it is the last resting place of Jews who died in Limerick, Kilkee, Newry and Belfast, and as far afield as Holyhead, Preston, Brighton, Manchester and Philadelphia. It was intriguing to hear that the Spanish and Portuguese consul in Holyhead, a Catholic by outward faith and a citizen of Portugal, requested in his will to be buried among Jews and was laid to rest in Ballybough.

Trades and Occupations

The majority of the Jews who came to Ireland came originally from eastern Europe. They took exotic, allusive names for themselves - Diamont, Rosenthal, Zlotover, Watchman - derived from precious stones and metals, poetic names and names referring to their trades and callings. When they arrived here they were taken charge of by the police and were housed with other foreigners; Italian organ-grinders, bear leaders, one-man band players and makers of saints of the Catholic Church. Many became pedlars of silks and tablecloths, hawking their wares around the back streets. They were known as "weekly" or "shilling a week men" because people bought their goods on the basis of paying a shilling a week for them.

They were obviously inventive people, founding what came to be known as hire purchase. Those with education, trades and artistic talent made a living as painters of miniatures, engravers, musicians, druggists, teachers of languages, pencil and chocolate makers and, of course, tailors. Elias Samuelson tailored the stage clothes of Vesta Tilley, a famous male impersonator and a Jewess.

As prejudice slowly disappeared, Jewish traders and merchants set up business to cater for the wealthy. They were cigar rollers and cigar importers, manufacturers of fancy sticks, umbrellas and Japanned cloth. They opened photographic galleries. Joseph Humphreys invented and patented brass, glass and transparent letters. A dentist on Grafton Street in Dublin advertised "Ingenious adaptation of Artificial Teeth by a method which involves no painful operation nor injurious fastening. A single tooth for five shillings, a complete set for five guineas."

Over time many Jews rose to prominence in the professions and in public life. Perhaps the most notable is Chaim Herzog, who was born in Belfast and became President of Israel. Robert Briscoe, the son of a Lithuanian immigrant, was a founder-member of the Fianna Fail party and was twice elected Lord Mayor of Dublin. His son Ben Briscoe is today a Fianna Fail T.D.

Integration into Irish society

I think it would be fair to say that Jewish emigrants to Ireland suffered to some extent from the stigma of difference and the suspicion and prejudice which that can evoke. They were supported in their request for tolerance and equal treatment by such leaders as Daniel O'Connell, Wolfe Tone and Michael Davitt. By and large they integrated and were accepted in 19th. century Irish society.

Friendliness with Catholic and Protestant neighbours existed. Prominent Christians would attend Jewish communal gatherings, prominent Jews were invited to receptions given by the Lord Lieutenant and the Lord Mayor. However, one particularly nasty incident did take place in Limerick. Around the turn of the century a Fr. Creagh indicted Jewish business and accused Jews of shedding Christian blood. Following his tirade from the pulpit, it is reported that the Jews of Limerick were insulted, assaulted and threatened with the most menacing language. Notwithstanding the fact that the priest's invective was generally condemned, a boycott instigated by him lasted two years and seriously undermined the Jewish community there. His superiors disowned him and he was withdrawn from Limerick. This sad episode, I am happy to say, was uncharacteristic and atypical.

Jewish Influences in Ulysses

In writing Ulysses, Joyce was concerned to present the true character of Dublin in 1904, which included an established Jewish population. Real life Jews with the name Bloom, living in Dublin at the time, make their appearance directly and indirectly in Ulysses. Marcus J. Bloom, a dentist on Clare Street, is an authentic character in the book. Jonas Bloom lived in 38 Lombard Street, which address Joyce also made Leopold Bloom's.

A nephew of Jonas, Simon Bloom was involved in a murder of a girl who worked in a photographer's shop in Wexford. She had jilted him and he vainly planned a double suicide. He was exonerated on mental grounds and after some time left for America.

Joyce, who was on a visit to Ireland around that time, would have read or heard about the incident and most likely formed the idea of making Leopold Bloom's daughter an apprentice in a photographer's shop. There was Daisy Bloom, a music teacher who converted to Catholicism. It is possible that Joyce knew of her and based aspects of Molly's character on her.

Leopold Bloom can be seen as the twentieth century symbol for Everyman. As R. P. Blackmur puts it, "Bloom is the wanderer, the movement and enterprise in Man, the thing immortal in society which persists from form to form. He is Everyman in exile, the exile in every man." Joyce asserted that in making the protagonist of Ulysses Jewish, he had placed the Jew on the map of European literature.

Jewish Registry of Deaths

How people die can sometimes tell us something more about the circumstances of their lives. The Jews in Ireland had large families. Unfortunately infant and child mortality was high. The chief causes of death were teething, croupe and scarletina. Causes of adult deaths included heart disease, consumption, typhoid fever, dysentery. The Jewish registry of deaths records causes such as - *Burnt to death by neglect of servant; After one day's illness; Suddenly; Drowned by accident in Liffey at North Wall* (Dublin's Wailing Wall it was known as, because of the sadness of emigration to South Africa for many Jews). There are curious entries such as, *Swelling in knee; Apoplexy; Insanity.* There was Consumption, of course, and Typhus Fever; a sad catalogue.

Through my research I had gained a limited knowledge of the Jewish community in 19th. century Ireland. I decided to let whoever of that community wished to, speak from the grave, affording us a unique and privileged insight into their lives.

JOSEPH PHILLIPS

Here I lie in Ballybough Cemetery
at the West Wall,
Row II, North to South,
buried in a white shroud.
Under my head,
turned slightly to face east,
a bag of earth from Israel.
You'd pass me by easily enough,
since I'm without a headstone.
Stolen, one drunken night,
it's serving as a hearthstone
in a house on nearby Richmond Road.
My grandson saw it there, poor boy,
while playing with his Catholic friend.
It reads –

Joseph Phillips, son of Uri. Native of Gorsd, Poland.
d. 6th. Kislev, 5640 (1879) aged 75.

That's me.
I made a living peddling wares
and selling pious pictures
to my Catholic neighbours.

ESTHER HARRIS

According to the registry of deaths
I died of insanity.
The locality was Brunswick Street North
in the year 1885 aged 39.
I have perfect clarity now,
the threatening voices are mollified
and lie quiet.
I sympathise with my plight back then —
the pogroms,
the arduous journey from Lithuania,
housed in a ghetto in Dublin in Chancery Lane
along with the Italian organ grinders,
and makers of saints of the Catholic Church.
Not a word of English between us.
The crushing homesickness!
I can see now why my mind went
as I craved the dark
in the house in North Brunswick Street,
red-bricked in the evening sun.

What a pity I missed out
on all those light-filled years.

GEORGE ISAACS

The death notice read,
died suddenly in mail packet
coming over from Liverpool.
Expelled from the congregation
for shameful conduct in synagogue,
I was on my way to Dublin
to marry out of the pale of Judaism,
as they termed it.
Poor Rose,
she turned up at the wailing North Wall
to greet a corpse.
The Elders' verdict on me was,
unrealistic, overly-romantic.
They were probably right,
but did they know how painful
I found life to be?

George Isaacs, died at sea.
That has a nice ring about it!

ALEXANDER ROSENSTEIN

A long name for someone
who was only in the world
for three years.
Burnt to death
by neglect of servant.
I did not understand
the strange smell from Maggie's breath
on the Sabbath when she was less tender
putting me to bed.
She lit the Shabbos candles.
They burned,
too close to the drapes.

Shivah candles should have flickered
in the house
for seven days after my death.
But who could light candles
after such a thing?

ABRAHAM ALTMAN

I was buried in a Christian cemetery
in Limerick,
but was quickly exhumed
and brought here by my brother.
I was brought here
not to suffer what was to come —
stones flung through windows,
the charge from the pulpit
that we would
kidnap and slay Christian children.
I was exhumed and brought by coach
not to hear the footsteps
of the last Jew living there.

Yet I remember the Festival of Lights
when hymns were sung
and children played spinning top
and a candle was lit each day
in the chanukah menorah
in the dark days of December,
while Christians, in the season of Advent,
lit four candles, one each Sunday,
in preparation for
the Light of the World.

REV. JULIUS SANDHEIM

Leaning over my Register
I recorded with great joy
the births of Jewish babies in Belfast.
Meir Levy's child was born in July 1849,
a time of terrible famine.
Frederick Samuel Boas,
who would become a distinguished
Shakespearean scholar,
was born in July 1862,
and the Jaffe children,
Egbert, Sarah, and Charles Sampson,
came soon after.
My private joy increased
with new births nearing a minyan,
the quorum of ten males
prescribed by Jewish law
for collective worship.

You see I had felt shamed.
A rabble with drums and riot
gathered outside Commercial Court in 1814,
and prevented a lecture on Hebrew Scriptures
by a solitary rabbi,
there being no Jews in the second city of Ireland
prior to that date.
I wished an end to shame.

WOLFE HERMAN

Cause of death, swelling in the knee.
Doctors, what do they know?
My heart,
it couldn't take any more!
My precious Sophie, she died,
my daughter, my only child!
She helped in the shop in Capel Street.
The customers all said,
"what big beautiful eyes, oh Wolfe
she'll break hearts."
Consumption took her from us.
And Bella, Bella my wife,
she could not live,
no point, she said.
I understood.
I kept the shop open.
The customers, my friends,
they were good to me.
Louis Harris, he had a bakery in Parliament Street.
We talked in the back room,
ate sponge cake and drank wine.
We laughed too.

But my heart, it broke.
Swelling in the knee,
doctors, what do they know?

JOSEPH LEVY

Tell me, why is it that a man,
reputedly a great wit,
leader of a synagogue,
a Councillor,
who knew the great joy
of a baby daughter in this new land,
lives to see her and her children
deserted by her husband Joseph Bloom
and to hear in the poisonous way of gossip
that she was seen with Bertha
her eldest daughter, my grandchild,
soliciting,
on the capital city's main street?

My daughter!
Tell me why is that?

JONAS BLOOM

I ask this question.
Did God plan a strategy of correction
when he saw me,
a neatly groomed man
with a gentle smile
and trimmed red beard,
wearing a frock-like coat and silk hat,
now with saddened eyes
and hands folded behind my back,
follow my pregnant, spinster daughter,
as she walked to and fro
in the cul-de-sac
beside our home,
dishevelled, of dubious repute,
mumbling maledictions?
Or did He merely observe?

Perhaps it is an impertinent question.
Perhaps I have no right to ask it.

SARAH LEVY

I take back my maiden name.
Joseph Bloom, my husband,
left me a grass widow
deserting me and our five children.
I took a Jewish lodger.
It happened I became his mistress.

Ostracised by the community,
a deserted wife, officially a widow,
I sold drapery to Jacob's factory girls
for a weekly payment.
A good looking woman,
in straitened circumstances,
where was I to turn?
To the streets,
myself, and worst of all,
Bertha my eldest.

DAISY BLOOM

Née Liknaitzky, I converted to Catholicism.
I picked up a copy of the Gospels
in a bookshop on the quays
and began to read.
Tears fell from my eyes
as I came to know Jesus Christ
for the first time.

I taught piano.
When alone,
I played, from time to time,
the Jewish songs of my childhood
with growing sadness
at what my people have not known —
The Lord, The Messiah.

SIMON BLOOM

Buried here,
again interned,
like the time I was confined
in a mental institution.
I had planned a double suicide.
She worked in a photographer's shop.
She jilted me, but
in my vanity,
I thought we both should die.
She died and I was exonerated
on mental grounds.

In this antechamber
I have the clarity of mind
I should have had
in life.

BENNY BLOOM

A veteran of the Boer War,
I marched the back streets of Dublin
armed with religious pictures.
Twenty miles a day was nothing to me.
I was a waiter and a bookie's runner too
and owned a gold mine in South Africa in my time.
I was fond of a drink
and always in financial straits,
eking out a living
purchasing old jewellery and gold.
A roué, by all accounts,
the "knee-trembler," they called me.
Mousy in appearance,
small and wiry,
well decked out in a check suit,
I wore a gold pin in my tie.

But Dublin would do the best man in.
She would draw out old sadnesses
and make failure look attractive
better than any city I ever lived in!

PESACH BLOOM

I was a "vikla man",
trading in silks and tablecloths
wrapped in a bundle
protected from the weather
by oil cloth.
I was hit by a falling slate
during The Big Wind in 1903
and died three months later, aged 49.

I should have stayed home
on a day that saw
the sturdiest of oaks in the Phoenix Park
laid low,
but I chose to carry
a burden on the shoulder
rather than a worry in the heart.

MOSES HERZOG

They owe me money.
They drank my tea
and ate my sugar
but did they pay me?
Now I will never collect.
They laughed at one-eyed Moishe Herzog,
needing to slip out for a drink
from the synagogue
during High Festival services.
Charged by law and ordered to pay me,
they say they report me
for having no licence to trade.
You drink my tea,
you eat my sugar,
you pay me!
What is more fair?

Now they never pay me!

MARCUS HARFMAN

In Cork I travelled in pictures,
my feet knowing every side alley,
dealing in the pennies and shillings
of that city
and bearing the jeers of children,
the drunk and the ignorant
but always thinking of my native land.
Although I was first buried here
in a Christian cemetery
the priest who attended me
witnessed my resolve
when I thrust aside the crucifix
he presented to me
and heard me utter a Hebrew prayer.

When I prayed that last time
I was back in the synagogue in Mitau.

SOLOMON MYERS

One by one my brothers left
for South Africa.
I saw them off at the North Wall.
My heart sank at each leaving.
After mamma and papa died
I walked down to the "Wailing Wall"
one night and slipped into the water.
It held me up as best it could
but in my best wool suit and leather boots
I sank down.
The death notice read,
Drowned by accident in Liffey at North Wall.

LEWIS HARRIS

I was a bill-broker and hard-nosed financier,
and the first Jew to enter public life in Ireland,
as Alderman of the South Dock Ward in Dublin.
On the 1st. of August 1876,
just before I was to be appointed Lord Mayor,
I passed away to the great regret
of Jew and Gentile alike, it seems.

In this black infinity,
what sticks in my mind is
a single rain drop in the sunlight,
after a summer shower.
Like that drop of rain,
falling from the supporting leaf,
I fell after a short illness.

REUBEN PHILLIPS

Buried in Ballybough cemetery,
in earth leased by my ancestor, Michael Phillips,
famous chocolate maker.
What will a man do with his life?
He should ask himself.
I was a grocer,
one of the two Jewish families,
living in Dublin in 1818.
I purchased fruit and vegetables
and sold them to my neighbours
for a small profit.
That is good.
But it is better that on the day the synagogue closed,
I took with me the *Megillah* for safe keeping
and bequeathed to the Community,
that book of prayer
and a *Sepher Torah*,
purchased for twenty guineas
three years before my death.
Twenty guineas! It was not easy.
A shilling here, a shilling there.
That much I did!

FRITZ MARIENHOFF

I spent my last days
in the Hospital of Incurables.
I was thirty-eight.
Doctor Harris did his best
on home visits.
A gentle man,
he said to me,
"you're young, healthy,
as far as I can see.
There is something 'though, Fritz,
what is it?"
Some months later
I passed through tall black gates;
Hospital of Incurables cut in stone.

A certain kind of heartbreak
is incurable.

"PENCIL" COHEN

Early disappointments in life
turned my soul.
In my tenement room
I turned to making ha'penny pencils
out of black lead.
Unable to spell my name or write my signature,
I amassed a great fortune,
but chose want and neglect for company.
I fried onions under the open window
to let the neighbours think
I have having steak for dinner.
Shame to say
I used old newspapers as bed sheets.
"Miser Cohen", they called me.

I was grieving early losses;
black lead on my fingers all day
and black ink-imprinted sheets at night.

NATHAN BENMOHEL

I lie here at Ballybough cemetery
listening to the racket of nesting rooks.
I lived my life in Sandycove,
divorced for many years
from the Congregation,
sleeping to the consoling shush of the sea.
I was brought here out of respect
for the wishes of my sister-in-law.
I had no part in that debate.
Although I am in good company —
Alderman Lewis Harris, lies close to me;
a Roman Catholic Consul is two rows down;
and Jacob Davis, teacher and lecturer
to the Congregation is on my left side —
I miss the sea.

On an especially silent night
if I strain my ears
I can hear the sound
of the incoming tide
at neighbouring Clontarf.

In death, as in life,
there is always consolation.

ALBERT GRANT

Born Abraham Zackariah
to a poor pedlar,
wrapped in charity swaddling clothes.
I fled the shameful scene
and rose by dint of graft and craft
to make London city a present —
of Leicester Square!
As "Baron" Grant,
pioneer of mammoth company promotion,
I was eventually exposed
a public swindler.
My last years were spent in legal actions.

I died, as I was born,
in poverty, in 1899.

DAVID ROSENBERG

What a life I had! —
the love of Martha,
five sons, all talented musicians,
Parnes of Mary's Abbey Synagogue,
and a nice greengrocer's business
in Charlemont Street.
I had my times of course,
at odds with my fellow man
and with the Almighty.
And I had an easy death.
What a thing,
to have my son the violinist
play the *Kol Nidre*,
as I atoned on my death bed.

With a peaceful heart,
after a long life,
I gave up the ghost.

GLOSSARY

chanukah	Feast of Lights
Kol Nidre	sacred melody traditionally sung on the eve of the Day of Atonement
Megillah	scroll telling the story of Esther and read on the Feast of Purim
menorah	candelabrum
minyan	a quorum of ten men required for prayer
Mitau	an old city in Poland
Parnes	President
Sephor Torah	scroll of the Law - the five Books of Moses
Shabbos	Hebrew for Sabbath
shivah	mourning

✡

42